PETE SEEGER
CENTENNIAL SONGBOOK

Words, Melody Line, and Chord Symbols

Photo by Charley Gallay/Getty Images

ISBN 978-1-5400-5384-8

TRO ESSEX
MUSIC GROUP

EXCLUSIVELY DISTRIBUTED BY

HAL•LEONARD®

Visit Hal Leonard Online at
www.halleonard.com

World headquarters, contact:
Hal Leonard
7777 West Bluemound Road
Milwaukee, WI 53213
Email: info@halleonard.com

In Europe, contact:
Hal Leonard Europe Limited
1 Red Place
London, W1K 6PL
Email: info@halleonardeurope.com

In Australia, contact:
Hal Leonard Australia Pty. Ltd.
4 Lentara Court
Cheltenham, Victoria, 3192 Australia
Email: info@halleonard.com.au

"I'm a link in a chain," Pete Seeger volunteered, in a long American tradition of singing for reform. Abolitionists, union organizers, civil rights, peace, and environmental activists – all turned to song to make their points.

For music captures the soul in ways that few political speeches can; it has encouraged and inspired revolutions. Realizing this, governments have tortured musicians like Victor Jara in Chile and Mikos Theodorakis in Greece, hoping to destroy a song by silencing its composer or performer.

In the United States, investigations of composers take the place of thumbscrews. Pete Seeger and his popular quartet, the Weavers have the distinction of being the only artists in American history formally investigated by the Senate for sedition and insurrection under Title 18, U. S. Code 2383-85 in the 1950s.

Pete could be found singing on a picket line or in a school auditorium or at a campfire as easily as he could singing in Carnegie Hall.

More than once, he set Carnegie Hall vibrating with the sound of thousands of voices singing in harmony. Few recordings capture his way of uniting strangers in song, and few know all that his campaigns cost his wife and family – the confiscated passports, the lost jobs, the personal attacks.

Pete Seeger's life resembled his song "Abiyoyo," an African folktale he adapted. It's the story of a boy and his musician father whom the town banishes for playing too loudly or too late at night. Then the Giant comes, and the boy defeats him. He doesn't fight him exactly. Instead of a stone, he uses a ukulele. The Giant dances until he's out of breath and falls down. Then the father whisks him away with his magic wand. The boy's music saves the town.

Now the town's elders can't remember why these great patriots shouldn't be at the head of the parade.

"Come back, bring your damn ukulele!" And the crowds welcome them and sing a song in their honor.

That Pete Seeger's father was run out of Berkeley's music department; that his son would bring his banjo to sing to his Congressional inquisitors – one doesn't need to know these things to decipher the parable. That music could help save a community from fascism or McCarthyism; that it's one of the forces uniting humanity – this was Pete Seeger's belief all along.

David King Dunaway
("How Can I Keep from Singing?
The Ballad of Pete Seeger"
Villard Books)

Here are a few of Pete's favorite songs – some he wrote, some his friends wrote. All are part of the folk process…

The Publisher

CONTENTS

THE MIDNIGHT SPECIAL

New Words and New Music Adaptation by
HUDDIE LEDBETTER
Edited by JOHN A. LOMAX and ALAN LOMAX

Additional Lyrics

2. Well, if you ever go to Houston,
Man, you'd better walk right.
And you had better not stagger,
And you'd better not fight,
Because the sheriff will arrest you,
He's gonna take you down.
And when the jury finds you guilty,
You're penitentiary bound.
Chorus

3. Well, yonder comes Miss Rosie.
How in the world did you know?
Well, I knew by her apron,
And the dress she wore.
Umbrella on her shoulder,
Piece of paper in her hand,
She goes a-marching to the captain,
Says, "I want my man."
Chorus

4. *(Pete Seeger's tribute verse)*
Old Huddie Ledbetter
He was a mighty fine man.
He taught us this song
And to the whole wide land.
But now he's done with all his grieving,
His whoopin', hollerin' and a-cryin'.
Now he's done with all his studyin'
About his great long time.
Chorus

IF I HAD A HAMMER
(The Hammer Song)

Words and Music by LEE HAYS
and PETE SEEGER

Additional Lyrics

3. If I had a song,
   I'd sing it in the morning;
   I'd sing it in the evening
    all over this land;
   I'd sing out danger,
   I'd sing out a warning,
   I'd sing out love between
    my brothers and my sisters,
   All over this land.

4. Well, I got a hammer,
   And I got a bell
   And I got a song to sing
    all over this land;
   It's the hammer of justice,
   It's the bell of freedom,
   It's the song about love between
    my brothers and my sisters,
   All over this land.

DEEP BLUE SEA

Traditional

Additional Lyrics

2. Dig his grave with a silver spade. (sing 3 times)
It was Willie what got drownded in the deep blue sea.
Chorus

3. Wrap him up in a silken shroud. (sing 3 times)
It was Willie what got drownded in the deep blue sea.
Chorus

4. Golden sun bring him back to me. (sing 3 times)
It was Willie what got drownded in the deep blue sea.
Chorus

WASN'T THAT A TIME?

Words and Music by LEE HAYS
and WALTER LOWENFELS

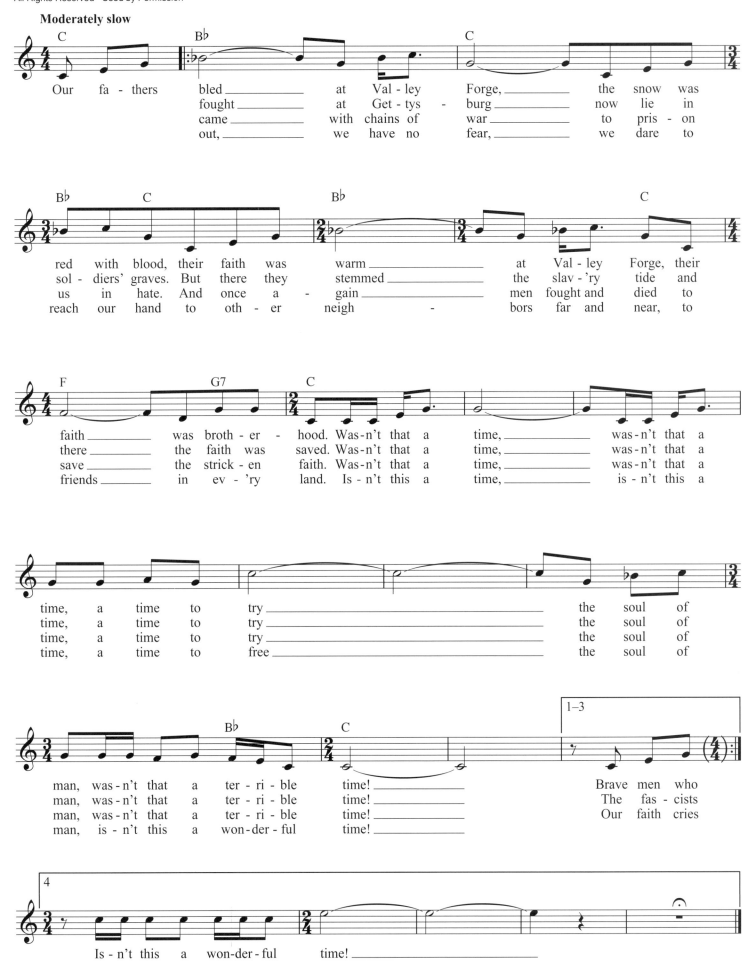

UNION MAID

Words and Music by WOODY GUTHRIE
Melody based on a traditional theme

Additional Lyrics

2. This union maid was wise to the tricks of company spies.
   She never got fooled by a company stool; she'd always organize the guys.
   She always got her way when she struck for higher pay.
   She'd show her card to the company guard, and this is what she'd say:
   Chorus

3. You gals who want to be free, just take a little tip from me:
   Get you a man who's a union man and join the Ladies' Auxiliary.
   Married life ain't hard when you've got a union card.
   A union man has a happy life when he's got a union wife.
   Chorus

WHAT DID YOU LEARN IN SCHOOL TODAY?

Words and Music by
TOM PAXTON

Moderately fast

Additional Lyrics

2. What did you learn in school today,
     dear little boy of mine? (Repeat)
   I learned that policemen are my friends,
   I learned that justice never ends,
   I learned that murderers die for their crimes
   Even if we make a mistake sometimes,
   And that's what I learned in school today,
   That's what I learned in school.

3. What did you learn in school today,
     dear little boy of mine? (Repeat)
   I learned our government must be strong,
   It's always right and never wrong,
   Our leaders are the finest men
   And we elect 'em again and again,
   And that's what I learned in school today,
   That's what I learned in school.

4. What did you learn in school today,
     dear little boy of mine? (Repeat)
   I learned that war is not so bad,
   I learned about the great ones we have had,
   We fought in Germany and in France,
   And some day I might get my chance,
   And that's what I learned in school today,
   That's what I learned in school.

LITTLE BOXES

Words and Music by
MALVINA REYNOLDS

Moderate Waltz tempo

Lit - tle box - es on the hill - side, lit - tle box - es made of tick - y tack - y; lit - tle
peo - ple in the hous - es, all went to the u - ni - ver - si - ty, where _
all play on the golf course, and drink their mar - ti - nis dry; and they
boys go in - to bus' - ness, and mar - ry and raise a fam - i - ly; and they

box - es on the hill - side, lit - tle box - es all the same. There's a
they were put in box - es, and they came out all the same. And there's
all have pret - ty chil - dren, and the chil - dren go to school. And the
all get put in box - es, lit - tle box - es all the same. There's a

green one, and a pink one, and a blue one, and a yel - low one; and they're
doc - tors, and there's law - yers, and bus' - ness ex - ec - u - tives; and they're
chil - dren go to sum - mer camp, and then to the un - i - ver - si - ty; where _
green one, and a pink one, and a blue one, and a yel - low one; and they're

all made out of tick - y tack - y, and they all look just the same.
all made out of tick - y tack - y, and they all look just the same.
they are put in box - es, and they all come out the same.
all made out of tick - y tack - y, and they all look just the

1–3

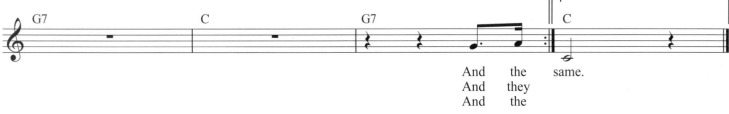

4

And the same.
And they
And the

WIMOWEH
(Mbube)

Words and Music by SOLOMON LINDA
Additional Words and Music by RONNIE GILBERT,
LEE HAYS, FRED HELLERMAN
and PETE SEEGER

A HARD RAIN'S A-GONNA FALL

Words and Music by
BOB DYLAN

Freely

1. Oh, where have you been, my blue - eyed __ son?
2.-5. *(See additional lyrics)*

And where have you been, my

dar - ling young one?

I've

stum - bled	on	the	side	of	twelve	mis - ty	moun - tains.
walked	and	I've	crawled	on	six	crook - ed	high - ways.
stepped	in	the	mid - dle	of	sev - en	sad	for - ests.
been	out	in	front	of	a	doz - en	dead	o - ceans.
ten	thou - sand	miles	in	the	mouth	of	a	grave - yard.

except final time

I've
I've
I've
I've been

final time

And it's a

hard, it's a hard, it's a hard,

it's a hard, it's a hard rain ____

____ s'a - gon - na fall. ____

1–4

5

D.C.

Additional Lyrics

2. Oh, what did you see, my blue-eyed son?
   And what did you see, my darling young one?
   I saw a newborn baby with wild wolves all around it
   I saw a highway of diamonds with nobody on it
   I saw a black branch with blood that kept dripping
   I saw a room full of men with their hammers a-bleeding
   I saw a white ladder all covered with water
   I saw ten thousand talkers whose tongues were all broken
   I saw guns and sharp swords in the hands of young children
   And it's a hard, it's a hard, it's a hard, and it's a hard
   It's a hard rain's a-gonna fall.

3. And what did you hear, my blue-eyed son?
   And what did you hear, my darling young one?
   I heard the sound of a thunder that roared out a warning
   I heard the roar of a wave that could drown the whole world
   I heard one hundred drummers whose hands were a-blazing
   I heard ten thousand whispering and nobody listening
   I heard one person starve, I heard many people laughing
   I heard the song of a poet who died in the gutter
   I heard the sound of a clown who cried in the alley
   And it's a hard, it's a hard, it's a hard, it's a hard
   It's a hard rain's a-gonna fall.

4. Oh, what did you meet, my blue-eyed son?
   And who did you meet, my darling young one?
   I met a young child beside a dead pony
   I met a white man who walked a black dog
   I met a young woman whose body was burning
   I met a young girl, she gave me a rainbow
   I met one man who was wounded in love
   I met another man who was wounded in hatred
   And it's a hard, it's a hard, it's a hard, it's a hard
   It's a hard rain's a-gonna fall.

5. And what'll you do now, my blue-eyed son?
   And what'll you do now, my darling young one?
   I'm a-going back out 'fore the rain starts a-falling
   I'll walk to the depths of the deepest dark forest
   Where the people are many and their hands are all empty
   Where the pellets of poison are flooding their waters
   Where the home in the valley meets the damp dirty prison
   And the executioner's face is always well hidden
   Where hunger is ugly, where the souls are forgotten
   Where black is the colour, where none is the number
   And I'll tell it and speak it and think it and breathe it
   And reflect from the mountain so all souls can see it
   Then I'll stand on the ocean until I start sinking
   But I'll know my song well before I start singing
   And it's a hard, it's a hard, it's a hard, and it's a hard
   It's a hard rain's a-gonna fall.

KISSES SWEETER THAN WINE

Words by RONNIE GILBERT, LEE HAYS,
FRED HELLERMAN and PETE SEEGER
Music by HUDDIE LEDBETTER

Additional Lyrics

3. I worked mighty hard and so did my wife,
   A-workin' hand in hand to make a good life.
   With corn in the fields and wheat in the bins,
   And then, oh, Lord, I was the father of twins.
   Chorus

4. Our children numbered just about four,
   And they all had sweethearts knock on the door.
   They all got married, and they didn't wait.
   I was, oh, Lord, the grandfather of eight.
   Chorus

5. Now we are old and ready to go.
   We get to thinkin' what happened a long time ago.
   We had lots of kids and trouble and pain,
   But, oh, Lord, we'd do it again.
   Chorus

IF IT CAN'T BE REDUCED

Words by MARTIN BOURQUE
Music by PETE SEEGER

GARDEN SONG

Words and Music by
DAVE MALLETT

Moderately

1., 4. Inch by inch, row by row, __ gon - na make this gar - den grow.
2., 3. (*See additional lyrics*)

All it takes is a rake and a hoe, and a piece of fer - tile ground. __

Inch by inch, row by row, __ some-one bless __ these seeds I sow. __

Some-one warm them from be - low __ till the rain comes tum - bl - ing down.

Additional Lyrics

2. Pulling weeds and picking stones, man is made of dreams and bones.
   Feel the need to grow my own 'cause the time is close at hand.
   Grain for grain, sun and rain, find my way in nature's chain.
   Tune my body and my brain to the music from the land.

3. Plant your rows straight and long, temper them with prayer and song.
   Mother Earth will make you strong if you give her love and care.
   Old crow watching hungrily from his perch in yonder tree.
   In my garden I'm as free as that feathered thief up there.

BLUE SKIES

Words and Music by
IRVING BERLIN

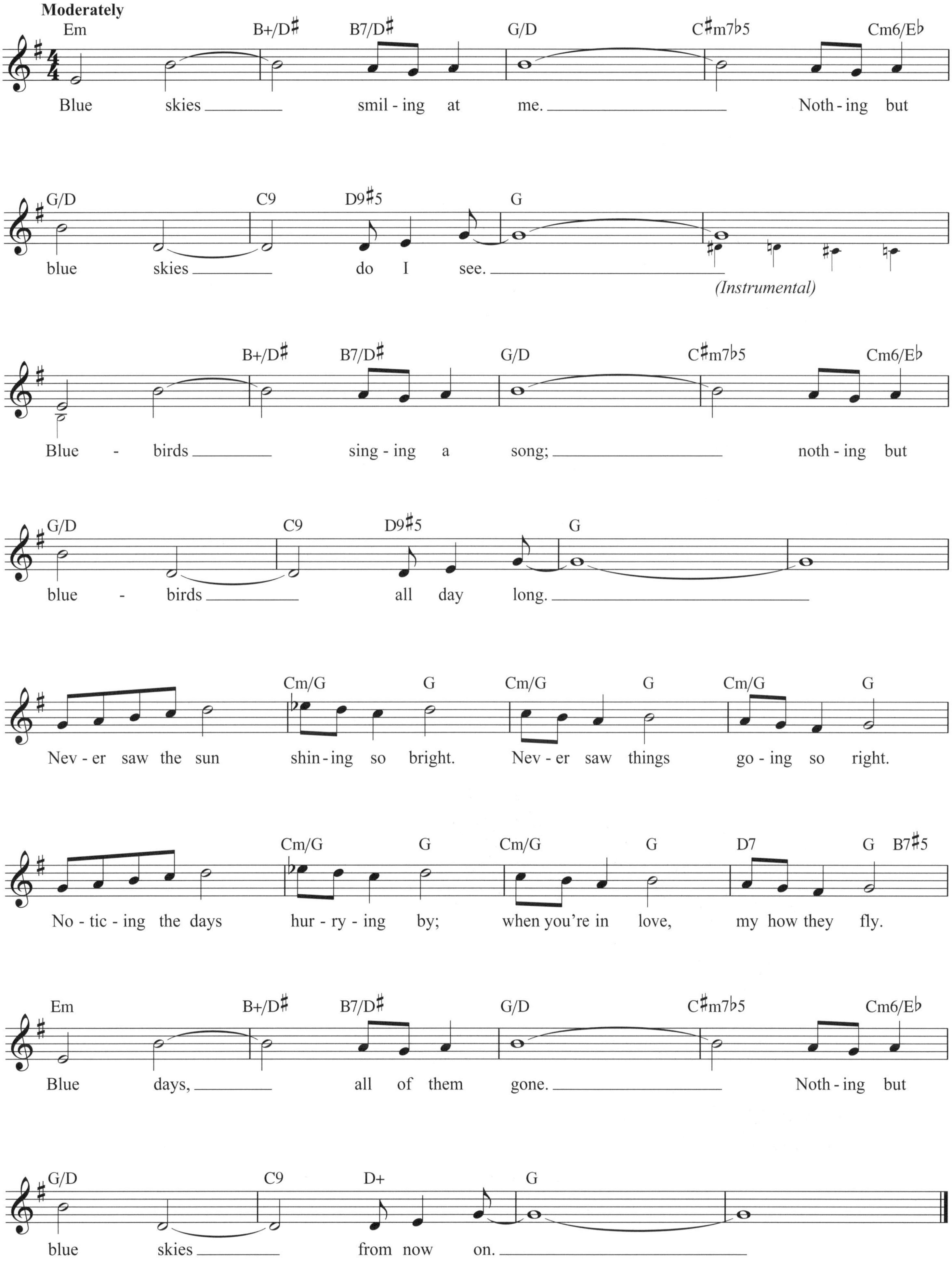

TURN! TURN! TURN!
(To Everything There Is a Season)

Words from the Book of Ecclesiastes
Adaptation and Music by PETE SEEGER

TURN! TURN! TURN!
(To Everything There Is a Season)
(The Byrds Version)

Words from the Book of Ecclesiastes
Adaptation and Music by PETE SEEGER

Additional Lyrics

2. A time to build up, a time to break down.
   A time to dance, a time to mourn.
   A time to cast away stones,
   A time to gather stones together.
   Chorus

3. A time of love, a time of hate.
   A time of war, a time of peace.
   A time you may embrace,
   A time to refrain from embracing.
   Chorus

4. A time to gain, a time to lose.
   A time to rend, a time to sew.
   A time for love, a time for hate.
   A time for peace; I swear it's not too late.
   Chorus

TURN! TURN! TURN!
(To Everything There Is a Season)
(Children's Version)

Words from the Book of Ecclesiastes
New Words by TOSHI SEEGER
Adaptation and Music by PETE SEEGER

Additional Lyrics

2. A time to dress, a time to eat
   A time to sit and rest your feet
   A time to teach, a time to learn
   A time for all to take their turn.
   Chorus

3. A time to cry and make a fuss
   A time to leave and catch the bus
   A time for quiet, a time for talk
   A time to run, a time to walk.
   Chorus

4. A time to get, a time to give
   A time to remember, a time to forgive
   A time to hug, a time to kiss
   A time to close your eyes and wish.
   Chorus

5. A time for dirt, a time for soap
   A time for tears, a time for hope
   A time for fall, a time for spring
   A time to hear the robins sing.
   Chorus

SNOW SNOW

Words and Music by
PETE SEEGER

Additional Lyrics

2. Under the street lamp, there stands a girl,
   Looks like she's not got a friend in this world.
   Look at the big flakes come drifting down,
   Twisting and turning, 'round and 'round.
   Chorus

3. Covers the mailbox, the farm and the plow,
   Even barbed wire seems – beautiful now.
   Covers the station, covers the tracks.
   Covers the footsteps of those who'll not be back.
   Chorus

SAILING DOWN MY GOLDEN RIVER

Words and Music by
PETE SEEGER

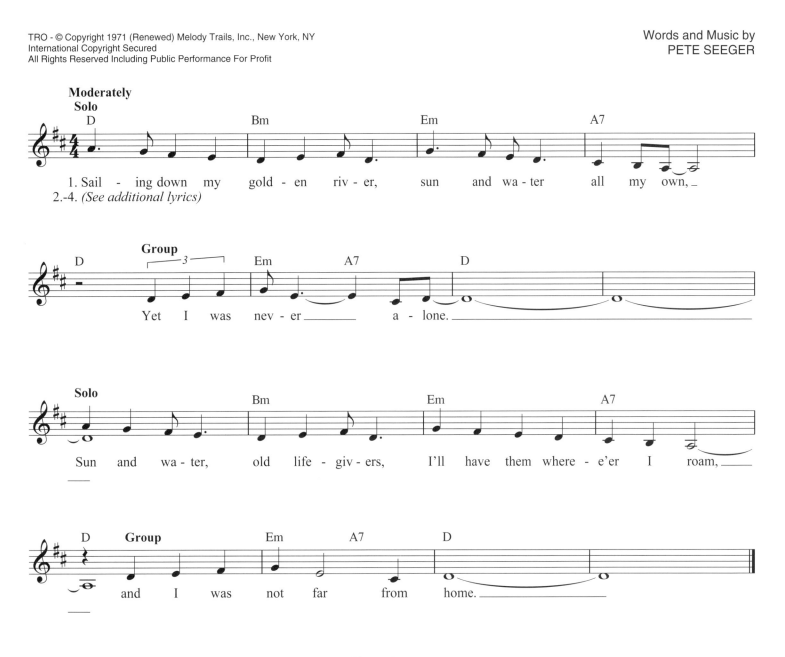

1. Sail - ing down my gold - en riv - er, sun and wa - ter all my own, _
2.-4. *(See additional lyrics)*

Yet I was nev - er _____ a - lone. _____

Sun and wa - ter, old life - giv - ers, I'll have them where - e'er I roam, _____

and I was not far from home. _____

Additional Lyrics

2. Sunlight glancing on the water
   Life and death are all my own
      And I was never alone.
   Life to raise my sons and daughters
   Golden sparkles in the foam
      And I was not far from home.

3. Sailing down this winding highway
   Travellers from near and far
      Yet I was never alone.
   Exploring all the little by-ways
   Sighting all the distant stars
      Yet I was not far from home.

4. Sailing down my golden river,
   Sun and water all my own,
      Yet I was never alone.
   Sun and water, old life-givers,
   I'll have them where'er I roam,
      And I was not far from home.

TALKING UNION

Words and Music by LEE HAYS,
MILLARD LAMPELL and PETE SEEGER

Moderately fast

1. If you want high-er wag-es, let me tell you what to do: you got to talk to the work-ers in the
2.-8. *(See additional lyrics)*

shop with you; __ you got to build you a un-ion, got to make it strong, __ but if you all stick to-geth-er, folks,

'twon't be long. You get short-er hours, __ Bet-ter work-ing con-di-tions.

Va-ca-tions with pay, __ take your kids to the sea-shore.

Additional Lyrics

2. It ain't quite this simple, so I better explain
   Just why you got to ride on the union train;
   'Cause if you wait for the boss to raise your pay,
   We'll all be waiting till Judgement Day;
   We'll all be buried – gone to Heaven –
   Saint Peter'll be the straw boss then.

3. Now, you know you're underpaid, but the boss says you ain't;
   He speeds up the work till you're 'bout to faint,
   You may be down and out, but you ain't beaten,
   Pass out a leaflet and call a meetin' –
   Talk it over – speak your mind –
   Decide to do something about it.

4. 'Course, the boss may persuade some poor damn fool
   To go to your meeting and act like a stool;
   But you can always tell a stool, though – that's a fact;
   He's got a rotten streak a-running down his back;
   He doesn't have to stool – he makes a good living –
   On what he takes out of blind men's cups.

5. You got a union now; you're sitting pretty;
   Put some people on the steering committee.
   The boss won't listen when just one squawks,
   But he's got to listen when the union talks.
   He better –
   He'll be mighty lonely one of these days.

6. Suppose he's workin' you so hard it's just outrageous,
   He's paying you all starvation wages;
   You go to the boss, and the boss would yell,
   "Before I raise your pay I'd see you all in Hell."
   Well, he's puffing a big see-gar and feeling mighty slick,
   He thinks he's got your union licked.
   He looks out the window, and what does he see
   But a thousand pickets, and they all agree
   He's a bastard – unfair – slave driver –
   Bet he beats his own wife.

7. Now, folks, you've come to the hardest time;
   The boss will try to bust your picket line.
   He'll call out the police, the National Guard;
   They'll tell you it's a crime to have a union card.
   They'll raid your meeting, hit you on the head.
   Call every one of you a doggone Red –
   Unpatriotic – Moscow agents –
   Bomb throwers, even the kids.

8. But out in Detroit here's what they found,
   And out in Frisco here's what they found,
   And out in Pittsburgh here's what they found,
   And down in Bethlehem here's what they found,
   That if you don't let Red-baiting break you up,
   If you don't let stool pigeons break you up,
   If you don't let vigilantes break you up,
   And if you don't let race hatred break you up –
   You'll win – What I mean –
   Take it easy – but take it.

MICHAEL, ROW THE BOAT ASHORE

Traditional

Moderately

Chorus

Michael, row the boat a-shore, Hal-le-lu - jah. Michael, row the boat a-shore, Hal-le-lu - jah.

1. Michael's
2.-4. *(See additional lyrics)*

Verse

boat is a mu-sic boat, Hal-le-lu - jah. Michael's boat is a mu-sic boat, Hal-le-lu - jah.

Additional Lyrics

2. Sister, help to trim the sail,
Hallelujah.
Sister, help to trim the sail,
Hallelujah.
Chorus

3. Jordan's River is deep and wide,
Hallelujah.
Meet my mother on the other side,
Hallelujah.
Chorus

4. Jordan's River is chilly and cold,
Hallelujah.
Kills the body but not the soul,
Hallelujah.
Chorus

OVER THE HILLS

Words by PETE SEEGER
Based on an Irish Folk Tune

Freely. *Best sung unaccompanied*

O-ver the hills I___ went one day, a-dream-ing of my-self and you, and the

spring-time of years since first we met___ and___ all___ that___ we've been through. May I

not with de-light still___ dream of the years of the sum-mer and fall___ to be? And the

man-y, man-y vers-es___ still to be sung in the bal-lad of you and me.

WAIST DEEP IN THE BIG MUDDY
(The Big Muddy)

Words and Music by
PETE SEEGER

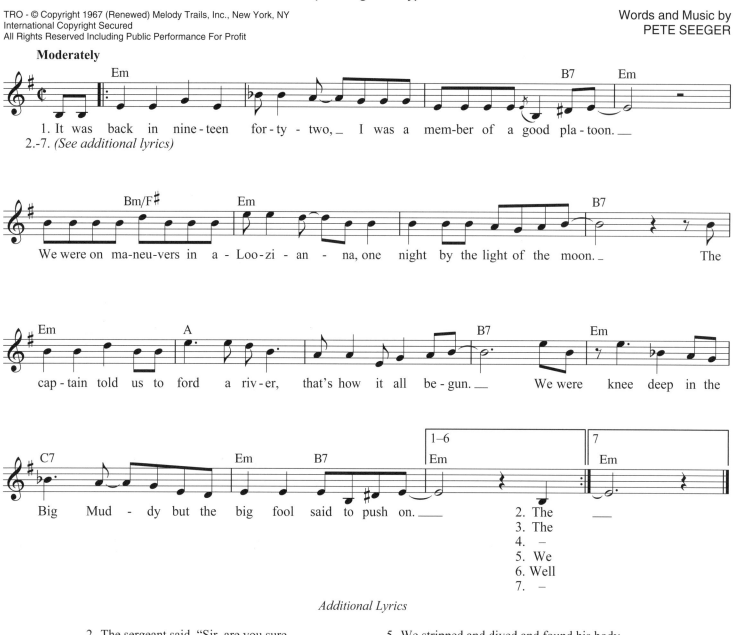

Moderately

1. It was back in nine-teen for-ty-two, __ I was a mem-ber of a good pla-toon. __
2.-7. *(See additional lyrics)*

We were on ma-neu-vers in a-Loo-zi-an-na, one night by the light of the moon. __ The

cap-tain told us to ford a riv-er, that's how it all be-gun. __ We were knee deep in the

Big Mud-dy but the big fool said to push on. ____

2. The
3. The
4. –
5. We
6. Well
7. –

Additional Lyrics

2. The sergeant said, "Sir, are you sure,
   This is the best way back to the base?"
   "Sergeant, go on; I forded this river
   'Bout a mile above this place
      It'll be a little soggy but just keep slogging.
      We'll soon be on dry ground."
      We were waist deep in the Big Muddy
      And the big fool said to push on.

3. The sergeant said, "Sir, with all this equipment
   No man'll be able to swim."
   "Sergeant, don't be a nervous Nellie,"
   The Captain said to him.
      "All we need is a little determination;
      Men, follow me, I'll lead on."
      We were neck deep in the Big Muddy
      And the big fool said to push on.

4. All at once, the moon clouded over,
   We heard a gurgling cry.
   A few seconds later, the Captain's helmet
   Was all that floated by.
      The sergeant said, "Turn around men,
      I'm in charge from now on."
      And we just made it out of the Big Muddy
      With the Captain dead and gone.

5. We stripped and dived and found his body
   Stuck in the old quicksand
   I guess he didn't know that the water was deeper
   Than the place he'd once before been.
      Another stream had joined the big Muddy
      'Bout a half a mile from where we'd gone.
      We were lucky to escape from the Big Muddy
      When the big fool said to push on.

6. Well, I'm not gonna point any moral;
   I'll leave that for yourself
   Maybe you're still walking and you're still talking
   And you'd like to keep your health.
      But every time I read the papers
      That old feeling comes on;
      We're waist deep in the Big Muddy
      And the big fool said to push on.

7. Waist deep in the Big Muddy
   And the big fool says to push on
   Waist deep in the Big Muddy
   And the big fool says to push on
      Waist deep! Neck deep!
      Soon even a tall man'll be over his head
      Waist deep in the Big Muddy!
      And the big fool said to push on!

WHERE HAVE ALL THE FLOWERS GONE?

Words and Music by
PETE SEEGER
with 4th and 5th verses by
JOE HICKERSON

Moderately slow, with simplicity

Additional Lyrics

3. Where have all the young men gone? Long time passing.
Where have all the young men gone? Long time ago.
Where have all the young men gone?
Gone for soldiers, every one.
When will they ever learn?
When will they ever learn?

4. Where have all the soldiers gone? Long time passing.
Where have all the soldiers gone? Long time ago.
Where have all the soldiers gone?
Gone to graveyards, every one.
When will they ever learn?
When will they ever learn?

5. Where have all the graveyards gone? Long time passing.
Where have all the graveyards gone? Long time ago.
Where have all the graveyards gone?
Covered with flowers, every one.
When will <u>we</u> ever learn?
When will <u>we</u> ever learn?

THE BELLS OF RHYMNEY

Words by IDRIS DAVIES
Music by PETE SEEGER

WE SHALL OVERCOME

Musical Adaptation and Arrangement by ZILPHIA HORTON,
FRANK HAMILTON, GUY CARAWAN and PETE SEEGER
Inspired by African American Gospel Singing,
members of the Food and Tobacco
Workers Union, Charleston, SC,
and the southern Civil Rights Movement

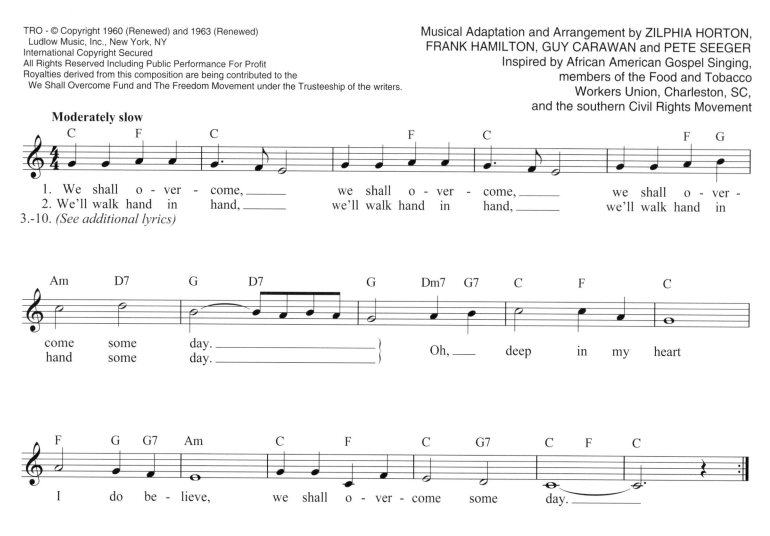

1. We shall o - ver - come, _____ we shall o - ver - come, _____ we shall o - ver -
2. We'll walk hand in hand, _____ we'll walk hand in hand, _____ we'll walk hand in
3.-10. *(See additional lyrics)*

come some day. _____
hand some day. _____ Oh, _____ deep in my heart

I do be - lieve, we shall o - ver - come some day. _____

Additional Lyrics

3. We are not afraid, we are not afraid,
   We are not afraid today,
   Oh, deep in my heart I do believe
   We shall overcome some day.

4. We shall stand together, we shall stand together,
   We shall stand together — now,
   Oh, deep in my heart I do believe
   We shall overcome some day.

5. The truth will make us free, the truth will make us free,
   The truth will make us free some day,
   Oh, deep in my heart I do believe
   We shall overcome some day.

6. The Lord will see us through, the Lord will see us through,
   The Lord will see us through some day,
   Oh, deep in my heart I do believe
   We shall overcome some day.

7. We shall be like *him*, we shall be like *him*,
   We shall be like *him* some day,
   Oh, deep in my heart I do believe
   We shall overcome some day.

8. We shall live in peace, we shall live in peace,
   We shall live in peace some day,
   Oh, deep in my heart I do believe
   We shall overcome some day.

9. The whole wide world around, the whole wide world around,
   The whole wide world around some day,
   Oh, deep in my heart I do believe
   We shall overcome some day.

10. We shall overcome, we shall overcome,
    We shall overcome some day,
    Oh, deep in my heart I do believe
    We shall overcome some day.

ALL MIXED UP

Words and Music by
PETE SEEGER

Moderately

1. You know, this lan-guage that we speak _ is part Ger-man, part Lat-in, and part Greek, _ with some
2.-4. *(See additional lyrics)*

Cel - tic and Ar - a - bic and Scan-di - na - vi - an all in the heap, well a-mend-ed by the

peo-ple in the street. Choc-taw gave us the word "O - kay," _ "Va-moose" is a word from

Mex-i - co way. _ And all of this is a hint, I sus - pect, _ of what comes next. _

Chorus

___ I think _ that this whole world, soon, _ ma - ma, my whole wide world,

soon, _ ma - ma, my whole world soon, _ gon - na be get mixed up.

Additional Lyrics

2. I like <u>Po</u>lish sausage, I like Spanish rice
 – Pizza pie is also nice
 <u>Corn</u> and beans from the Indians here
 <u>Wash</u>ed down by some German beer
 <u>Marco</u> Polo traveled by camel and pony
 – Brought to Italy the first macaroni
 And <u>you</u> and I, as well as we're able
 – Put it all on the table.
 I think that this
 Chorus

3. There <u>were</u> no redheaded Irishmen
 Before the <u>Vik</u>ings landed in Ireland.
 <u>How</u> many Romans had dark curly hair
 <u>Be</u>fore they brought slaves from Africa?
 No <u>race</u> on earth is completely pure;
 Nor is <u>any</u>one's mind and that's for sure.
 The <u>winds</u> mix the dust of every land,
 And <u>so</u> will woman and man.
 No chorus

4. Oh, <u>this</u> doesn't mean we will all be the same.
 We'll have <u>diff</u>erent faces and different names.
 <u>Long</u> live many different kinds of races
 And <u>diff</u>erence of opinion; that makes horse races.
 Just re<u>mem</u>ber The Rule About Rules, brother:
 "What's <u>right</u> with one is wrong with another."
 <u>And</u> take a tip from La Belle France,
 – "Vive la difference."
 I think that this
 Chorus

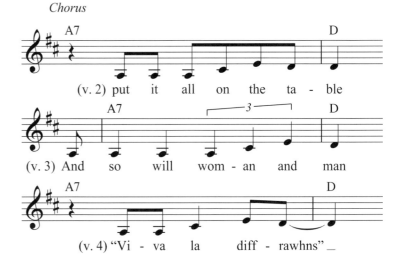

(v. 2) put it all on the ta - ble

(v. 3) And so will wom - an and man

(v. 4) "Vi - va la diff - rawhns" _

* *This irregularity, a 6/4 measure, is only in the first verse.*
 The rest of the verses hold to ₵ time.
** *See variant melodies for the last line of verses 2, 3, and 4.*

SOLARTOPIA

Words and Music by PETE SEEGER,
DAVID BERNZ and HARVEY WASSERMAN

Additional Lyrics

2. We bit that apple and the Garden was lost
So we had to work to pay the cost
And so we went digging into the ground
And started to burn many things we found, but...
Chorus

3. We multiplied and we needed more
The rich got rich, the poor got sore
The fuel ran scarce, the price jumped high
And so we gave nuclear power a try, but...
Chorus

4. But the nuclear plants were built in haste
With too many risks, no place for waste
And so from Seabrook to Shoreham town
We have to shut those nuke plants down.
Chorus

5. Now we're fighting wars over oil and gas
No matter who wins, it will not last
The earth is scarred, the planet is warming
Don't you think that all of it's a great big warning?
Chorus

6. We'll learn to power houses and cars
With the light that's made up in stars
It's a gift to share that's always been given
It falls down to Earth like rain from Heaven.
Chorus

This song was written in support of the book "Solartopia" written by Harvey Wasserman. It sets forth a 30-year blueprint for a nuclear-free, fossil fuel-free solar and wind powered world. See: solartopia.org.

ONE GRAIN OF SAND

Words and Music by
PETE SEEGER

Slowly, freely and tenderly

1. One grain of sand, _____ One grain of sand, _____ in
2.-11. *(See additional lyrics)*

all the world, One grain of sand, _____ One lit - tle boy, one lit-tle girl. _

Additional Lyrics

2. One grain of sand,
   One lonely star up in the blue,
   One grain of sand,
   One little me, one little you.

3. One grain of sand,
   One grain of sand on an endless shore,
   One grain of sand,
   One little life, who'd ask for more?

4. One grain of sand,
   One drop of water in the sea,
   One grain of sand,
   One little you, one little me.

5. One grain of sand,
   One grain of sand is all my joy,
   One grain of sand,
   One little girl, one little boy.

6. One grain of sand,
   One leaf of grass upon a plain,
   One grain of sand,
   We come and go again and again and again.

7. One grain of sand,
   One little snowflake lost in a swirling storm,
   One grain of sand,
   I'll hold you close and keep you warm.

8. The sun will rise,
   The sun will rise and then go down,
   The sun will rise,
   One little world go round and round and round.

9. So close your eyes,
   So close your eyes and go to sleep,
   So close your eyes,
   One little smile, one little weep.

10. One grain of sand,
    One grain of sand is all my own,
    One grain of sand,
    One grain of sand is home sweet home.

11. So go to sleep,
    So go to sleep by the endless sea,
    So go to sleep,
    I'll hold you close, so close to me.

SO LONG IT'S BEEN GOOD TO KNOW YUH
(Dusty Old Dust)

Words and Music by
WOODY GUTHRIE

Dust Bowl Version

A dust storm hit, and it hit like thunder,
It dusted us over and it covered us under;
Blocked out the traffic and blocked out the sun.
Straight for home all the people did run.
Chorus

The sweethearts, they sat in the dark and they sparked.
They hugged and they kissed in that dusty old dark.
They sighed and they cried, they hugged and they kissed,
Instead of marriage, they talked like this: Honey,
Chorus

Now, the telephone rang and it jumped off the wall;
That was the preacher a-making his call.
He said, "Kind friend, this may be the end;
You've got your last chance of salvation of sin."
Chorus

The churches was jammed, and the churches was packed,
And that dusty old dust storm blowed so black;
The preacher could not read a word of his text;
And he folded his specs and he took up collections, said:
Chorus

Weavers Version

The sweethearts, they sat in the dark and they sparked.
They hugged and they kissed in that dusty old dark.
They sighed and they cried, they hugged and they kissed,
Instead of marriage, they talked like this: Honey,
Chorus

I went to your fam'ly, I asked them for you.
They all said, "Take her, oh, take her, please do!
She can't cook or sew and she won't scrub the floor,"
So I put on my coat, tiptoed out of the door, saying:
Chorus

I walked down the street to the grocery store.
It was crowded with people both rich and both poor.
I asked the man how his butter was sold;
He said, "One pound of butter for two pounds of gold," I said:
Chorus

Now, the telephone rang and it jumped off the wall;
That was the preacher a-making his call.
He said, "We're waitin' to tie the knot;
You're gettin' married, believe it or not!"
Chorus

The church, it was jammed, and the church, it was packed,
The pews were crowded from the front to the back.
A thousand friends waited to kiss my new bride,
But I was so anxious I rushed her outside. Told them:
Chorus

JOE HILL

Words and Music by EARL ROBINSON
and ALFRED HAYES

GUANTANAMERA

Musical Adaptation by PETE SEEGER and JULIÁN ORBÓN
Lyric Adaptation by JULIÁN ORBÓN,
based on a poem by JOSÉ MARTÍ
Lyric Editor: HECTOR ANGULO
Original Music and Lyrics by JOSÉ FERNÁNDEZ DIAZ

Additional Lyrics

2. Mi verso es de un verde claro
Y de un carmín encendido
Mi verso es de un verde claro
Y de un carmín encendido
Mi verso es un ciervo herido
Que busca en el monte amparo
Chorus

3. Con los pobres de la tierra
Quiero yo mi suerte echar
Con los pobres de la tierra
Quiero yo mi suerte echar
El arroyo de la sierra
Me complace más que el mar.
Chorus

English translation of verses

1. I am a truthful man,
From the land of the palms.
Before dying, I want to
Share these poems of my soul.

2. My poems are light green,
But they are also flaming red.
My verses are like a wounded fawn,
Seeking refuge in the mountain.

3. With the poor people of this earth,
I want to share my lot.
The little streams of the mountains
Please me more than the sea.

MY RAINBOW RACE

Words and Music by
PETE SEEGER

And be-cause I love you, _____ I'll _____ give it one more try, _____
To show my rain - bow race _____ It's too soon to die.
Go tell, go tell all _____ the lit-tle chil-dren, Tell all the moth-ers and fa-thers too, _____
Now's our last chance _ to learn to share _what's been giv - en to me and you. One blue sky! Sing it!
One blue sky a - bove us, One o-cean lap-ping all our shore,
One earth so green and round, _ Who could ask for more?

LONESOME VALLEY

New Words and New Music Adaptation by
WOODY GUTHRIE

Moderately

1. You got to walk _____ that lone - some val - ley, _____ you got to
2.-4. *(See additional lyrics)*

walk _____ it by your - self. _____ No-bod - y here _____ can walk it

for you, _____ you got to walk _____ it by your - self.

Additional Lyrics

2. Daniel was a Bible hero,
   Was a prophet brave and true.
   In a den of hungry lions
   He showed what faith can do for you.

3. Some folks say that John was a Baptist,
   Some folks say he was a Jew
   But the holy Bible tells us
   That he was a preacher too.

4. Now though the road be rough and rocky,
   And the hills be steep and high,
   We can sing as we go marching,
   And we'll win that one big union by and by.

SYLVIE
(Bring Me Li'l' Water, Silvy)

Words and Music by HUDDIE LEDBETTER,
RONNIE GILBERT, LEE HAYS,
FRED HELLERMAN and PETE SEEGER
Collected and adapted by
JOHN A. LOMAX and ALAN LOMAX

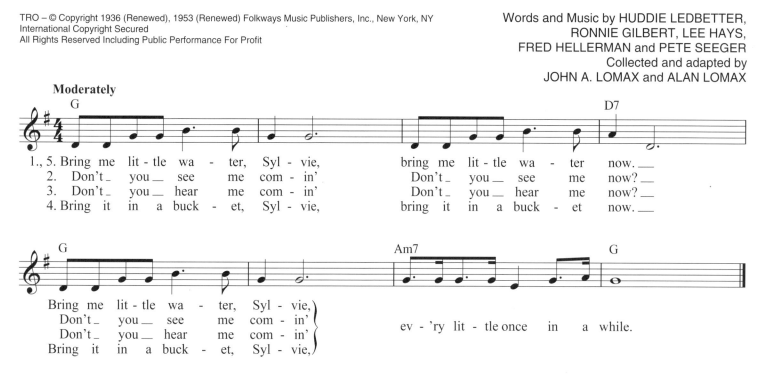

1., 5. Bring me lit-tle wa-ter, Syl-vie, bring me lit-tle wa-ter now. __
2. Don't_ you_ see me com-in' Don't_ you_ see me now? __
3. Don't_ you_ hear me com-in' Don't_ you_ hear me now? __
4. Bring it in a buck-et, Syl-vie, bring it in a buck-et now. __

Bring me lit-tle wa-ter, Syl-vie,
Don't_ you_ see me com-in'
Don't_ you_ hear me com-in'
Bring it in a buck-et, Syl-vie, } ev-'ry lit-tle once in a while.

GET UP AND GO

Words collected, adapted and set to Original Music by
PETE SEEGER

How do I know my youth is all spent, my get up and go has
got up and went. But in spite of it all I'm a-ble to grin and
think of the plac-es my get up has been.

Old age is gold-en,
When I was young my

so I've heard said, but some-times I won-der as I crawl in-to bed. With my
slip-pers were red, I could kick up my heels right ov-er my head.

ears in a draw-er, my teeth in a cup, my eyes on the ta-ble, un-
When I was old-er my slip-pers were blue, but still I could dance the

WHICH SIDE ARE YOU ON?

Words and Music by
FLORENCE REECE

Which side are you on, boys? Which side are you on? __ on? 1.They say in Har-lan coun-ty,there are no neu-trals there._You'll ei-ther be a un-ion man or a thug for J. H. Blair.(Chorus)

2.-4. *(See additional lyrics)*

Additional Lyrics

2. My daddy was a miner, and I'm a miner's son.
   He'll be with your fellow workers until this battle's won.
   Chorus

3. O workers can you stand it? O tell me how you can.
   Will you be a lousy scab or will you be a man?
   Chorus

4. Come all of your good workers, good news to you I'll tell
   Of how the good old Union has come in here to dwell.
   Chorus

OH, HAD I A GOLDEN THREAD

Words and Music by
PETE SEEGER

1.,6. Oh,_____ had I a gold-en thread, ___ and nee-dle_ so fine, _____

2.-5. *(See additional lyrics)*

___ I'd _____ weave a mag-ic strand ___ of rain-bow_ de-sign, _____

___ of ___ rain-bow _____ de - sign. _____

Additional Lyrics

2. In it I'd weave the bravery
   Of women giving birth,
   In it I would weave the innocence
   Of children over all the earth,
   Children of all earth.

3. Far over the waters
   I'd reach my magic band
   Through foreign cities,
   To every single land,
   To every land.

4. Show my brothers and sisters
   My rainbow design,
   Bind up this sorry world
   With hand and heart and mind,
   Hand and heart and mind.

5. Far over the waters
   I'd reach my magic band
   To every human being
   So they would understand,
   So they'd understand,

WE'LL ALL BE A-DOUBLING

Words by PETE SEEGER
Music: Traditional

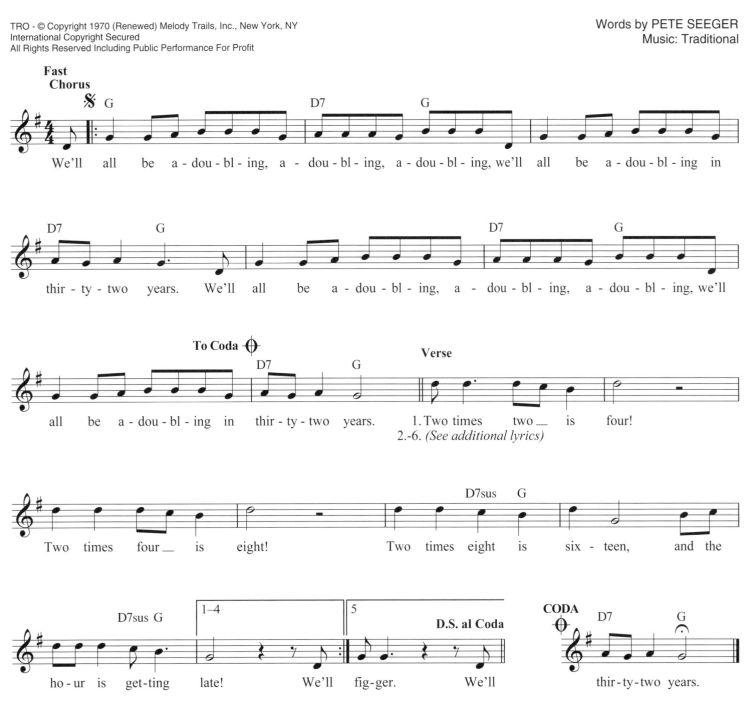

Additional Lyrics

2. Twice sixteen is thirty-two.
Next comes sixty-four.
Next a hundred and twenty-eight.
Do we need to hear more?
Chorus

3. Next is two hundred fifty-six.
Next five hundred and twelve.
Next one thousand and twenty-four.
So figure it out yourself.
Chorus

4. Keep doubling ten generations.
You can have children over a million.
Keep going another twenty.
Your children would be over a trillion.
Chorus

5. Either people gonna have to get smaller
Or the world's going to have to get bigger;
Or there's a couple other possibilities,
I'll leave it to you to figger.
Chorus

TOMORROW IS A HIGHWAY

Words by LEE HAYS
Music by PETE SEEGER

A song for the new year and a new day. Try it with altos and basses taking the melody, sopranos and tenors the harmony.

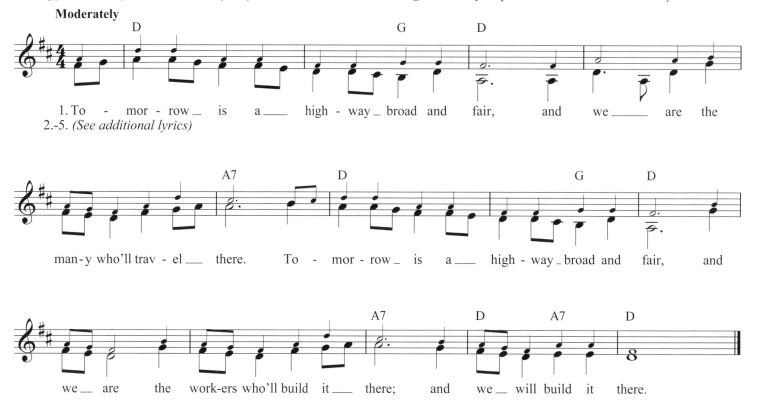

1. To - mor - row _ is a _ high - way _ broad and fair, and we _ are the
2.-5. *(See additional lyrics)*

man - y who'll trav - el _ there. To - mor - row _ is a _ high - way _ broad and fair, and

we _ are the work - ers who'll build it _ there; and we _ will build it there.

Additional Lyrics

2. Come, let us build a way for all mankind.
   A way to leave this evil year behind,
   To travel onward to a better year
   Where love is, and there will be no fear,
   Where love is, and no fear.

3. Now is the shadowed year when evil men,
   When men of evil thunder war again.
   Shall tyrants once again be free to tread
   Above our most brave and honored dead?
   Our brave and honored dead.

4. O, comrades, come and travel on with me,
   We'll go to our new year of liberty.
   Come, walk upright, along the people's way,
   From darkness, unto the people's day.
   From dark to sunlit day.

5. Tomorrow is a highway broad and far
   And hate and greed shall never travel there
   But only they who've learned the peaceful way
   Of brotherhood, to greet the coming day.
   We hail the coming day.

GOODNIGHT, IRENE

Words and Music by HUDDIE LEDBETTER
and JOHN A. LOMAX

Additional Lyrics

2. Sometimes I live in the country,
   Sometimes I live in town.
   Sometimes I take a great notion
   To jump into the river and drown.
   Chorus

3. Stop ramblin', stop your gamblin',
   Stop staying out late at night.
   Go home to your wife and fam'ly,
   Stay there by your fireside bright.
   Chorus

4. I asked your mother for you,
   She told me you was too young.
   I wish to God I never seen your face,
   I'm sorry you ever was born.
   Chorus

5. You caused me to weep and you caused me to moan,
   You caused me to leave my home.
   The last words I heard her say,
   "I want you to sing me a song."
   Chorus

THIS LAND IS YOUR LAND

Words and Music by
WOODY GUTHRIE

Additional Lyrics

2. I've roamed and rambled and I followed my footsteps
   To the sparkling sands of her diamond deserts.
   And all around me, a voice was sounding,
   "This land was made for you and me."
   Chorus

3. When the sun came shining, and I was strolling,
   And the wheat fields waving and the dust clouds rolling.
   As the fog was lifting, a voice was chanting,
   "This land was made for you and me."
   Chorus

4. As I went walking, I saw a sign there.
   And on the sign it said "No Trespassing."
   But on the other side it didn't say nothing.
   That side was made for you and me.
   Chorus

5. In the shadow of the steeple I saw my people.
   By the relief office I seen my people.
   As they stood there hungry, I stood there asking:
   Is this land made for you and me?
   Chorus

6. Nobody living can ever stop me,
   As I go walking that freedom highway.
   Nobody living can ever make me turn back.
   This land was made for you and me.
   Chorus

TO MY OLD BROWN EARTH

Words and Music by
PETE SEEGER

WELL MAY THE WORLD GO

Words and Music by
PETE SEEGER

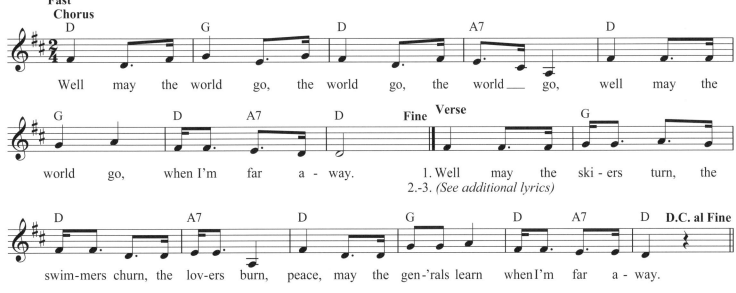

Additional Lyrics

2. Sweet may the fiddle sound
   The banjo play the old hoe down
   Dancers swing 'round and 'round
   When I'm far away.
   Chorus

3. Fresh may the breezes blow
   Clear may the streams flow
   Blue above, green below
   When I'm far away.
   Chorus

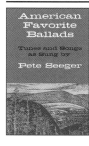

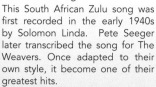